Not a Myth

THE FAOINSGEUL WOODS

MOLLY LIKOVICH

MARCIA RUIZ-OLGUÍN

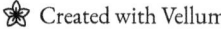

For the bees, forever and always.

Am I magic enough for you, my love? Am I real?

— CARAVAN OF LIES

INTO THE WOODS

"Out beyond ideas of wrongdoing and rightdoing there is a field. I'll meet you there."
-Rumi

The sun is sinking in the sky as staircases wind
towards a beautiful unknown.
Is this where you get lost?
Do you remember those bygone days of witches
and hobgoblins and stories you learned
to deem false?
Are your eyes weak from the sun on Sundays,
kneeling before gods you stopped
believing in long ago?

There are altars there.
Did you know that once the world
was one giant forest? Woods covered
this earth from coast to coast. A never-ending
nightmare of beautiful darkness.
No one had hylophobia because no one
knew how to fear the only home they'd ever known. You can follow

the milky white rabbit deep into the stories
you wish you hadn't grown out of, like an old
sweater you dug out from under the bed.
There's a wildness in you that churches gnash their
teeth at—wishing they could tame.
Wine should be drunk for more than holy reasons.
Are you coming?
This is only the beginning.

You know, they say if you find a staircase

in the woods you should never climb it.

HAUNTED AIR

Deep in these woods, there is a place
for the wandering. Maybe

a simple arch made of forest. Maybe
coated in so many gold flourishes you
can hardly see the old rotting
wood underneath. Some smell

like sea salt breezes or star-laden
skies. Some

wanderers simply stepped into
faery rings and fell through
the earth to a place of poisoned
fruit and salted stories you wouldn't dare tell.

Some dove deep enough
into murky waters until mermaids
led the way to a kingdom

of impossibles and forevers
and throats that can swallow
salt water and turn it into song.

Some merely meant
to hang up their coat, wet from
the rain, only to find themselves
inside a faery tale.

Some walk until the road ends

and then they keep going.

Perhaps some lead to worrisome worlds but more lead
to a marvelous

maddening magic
you can only taste in your dreams.

A PIECE OF POETRY FOUND FLOATING IN A RIVER SOMEWHERE

no matter what the stories tell you,
the living cannot kill the ghosts, and the ghosts cannot trust the living.
people

    see them, by the river—floating in dresses of black and
    white. they make waves and people see
    stars and the tombstones dance under the moon.

        but these are just stories.
        and they were just girls.

WISE WORDS FROM THE WOMEN IN THE BOTHAN

Lichen lines the walls; no one ever believes us
when we tell them that the sea can reach us
here. Crash through our cottage doors soaking us through with
honey, with the buzz of bees, with the swinging of swords and
the jingling of keys.

No one ever believes us.

You have the heart, you wear the key, and if you look long
enough, you will carry the feather. Go

deeper. Pick the door no one else thinks to look for. Your mind
is better equipped for choosing than the others. They've all
been waiting so long for you.

Some are up above, popping champagne, dancing in seas of glit-
ter. Down here, deep in the woods, we count rabbits instead of
minutes. We smash the berries she uses for her paint.

Have you seen the painting yet? You have. We can see it on you.
The gold
is all over your heart.

If you need a better look at the path you are bound
to take, go to the roof. Be mindful of the mushrooms and flow-
ers; magic beans in every color, and set your sights on all the
ways your heart can get lost out there, and your mind can go off
after it.

Have you chosen your path? Yes? Good. Now come inside for a
bit. It's very cold out and we've made tea.
You can leave in the morning.

WHAT LURKS IN THE DARK

"Come inside, it's going to rain."
-Caravan of Lies

The Mother

I know all the herbs we need to see all the stories
we need
to know. I know all the ways to love even the most
foolish things. I make my magic look
practical. I let the rain
beat sense into the senseless.
But I've never turned a wanderer away.

The Maiden

I have tea for that. Flowers to mend. I have
every impossibility and I know how to make
them fit inside
the curves of a teacup.
I can show you every road you need
to wander. I can make the rain
listen. I can
see in the dark.

The Crone

No one knows
who I am. Cave walls and palaces.
The curse of forever.
That is the price of becoming a thing of legend;

of swallowing mythology

and making it a part of yourself.

I am not afraid of what lurks in the dark.
I am the thing they should fear.

FIACLAN

*"There's something wrong with us. I feel it sometimes; something rotten on
the inside."*
-'House of Hollow' by Krystal Sutherland

There are over 400,000 people in the city where we lost our skin. The
cobblestoned street where we stumbled into the land of the dead. Of
gray berries and gray skies

and horns and things that make children scream. She sewed us up nice
and neat. Moon marks on our throats. *Don't tell your story*, is what she
whispered before

we forgot. Beautiful ignorance, as rancid as the flowers rotting under
our skin. She is still all bones and beauty. I've never stopped wishing I
could be her.

Maybe she stitched me into the wrong skin. Screwed the wrong teeth
into my gums. Called me monster
when I'm really just a mouse. I think she could kill

us too if she really wanted to. Peel our skins back
like oranges and peaches and apples and all things
that juice and bleed. Maybe we'd say thank you

Maybe I'd finally bite her. Maybe I'd tear my
flesh myself just to see the flowers blooming
where my veins should be. Gaze at the rough muscle

and white bone that once called itself Hollow. I took that name, didn't
I? Put it on just like this skin and
said it was mine. Except that I didn't

She wrapped me up in it and told me to forget.
Forget the gray and the house and all the things
with horns so big they block out the stars

She dragged us back into the city of 400,000
people with teeth so much duller than ours.

LIVELY

Buzz cut. Hair bleached. Nothing makes
any sense anymore. It never
did. There's a garden inside me.

It's rotting. Putrid. Rancid. It's all
make believe. Just a story we
tell our little sister. We sewed

the world up with thread and called
ourselves perfect. Complete. Human.
We are bones and blood. Our throats

hold siren song, our touch sticks
like honey. Our prey can never wash
themselves of us. Once we've
touched—

we stain. I think
someone hurt us once. Made us
moon shaped. Made us scared.

Sometimes I remember naked
limbs shaking on cobblestone
streets and I wonder what made us.

What are we made of? Fairytales?
Gardens? Nightmares.

BEAUTIFUL BEASTS

They were so cold and I was
so strong. Needle and thread.
I fit entire universes under skin.

Tucked legacies between bones.
I gave them everything. Death
is such a small cost, we made sure

there was no one to miss. Teeth
on teeth and skin on skin. Rancid
flowers and honey-silk breath.

Words that can wound and wind
and command and capture. Words
that can torture if needed. Who

wouldn't want to be us? Why
wouldn't my darling sisters
adore me? I made them into myths.

I made them into things that
could be great. Monsters in
gold dresses. Beautiful beasts,

cloaked in colorful, rotting flowers.
Together we made the most
grotesque work of art. I won't

let anyone take it all away.

A LETTER FROM THE WIDOW AT THE STONE

-after ivy by taylor swift

the wine has almost been drunk
and the fire is getting low.
i tried calling out to you. i made my voice

birdsong. wove it into the snow.
but your stones are strong. i'm sure
from where you stand

my world looks coraline-dreamed.

something the painters go blind
for. i assure you, i had fireside lovers too.
some things are simply worth burning for.

NEVER IS AN AWFULLY LONG TIME

Could be a fairy ring in a clearing in the middle of the unspoken, unentered woods. Could be an archway covered in vines grown since the time the Gods walked the earth. Or it could be a good, old fashioned door. It could be painted in rich golds and blues, woven with the smell of dreams and melted caramel and topped with fresh tangy honey.

Or perhaps the wood is rotted and worn. Creaking like a dying man craving water to slick his scratchy throat. Maybe it hisses with a horrendous screech like nails on a chalkboard; the hinges whining like a cat in an alley.

Regardless, it is undoubtedly beautiful. Ridiculously magnificent. Absolutely, positively, most ardently extraordinary in every way.

Will you open it? She painted it just for you. All you have to do

is grasp the knob, and turn, and disappear. Never to return.

Sorry this is so packed today

WONDROUS

She's not really
a person. She's
something more.

A bag full of stories,
tongue heavy with
tales. Did you think

you were her friend?
She clipped owls'
wings and slashed

at valiant hearts. She screamed
a universe into existence.
Honey-heavy and lives

long. Her hair, the color
of love; but can a dying thing
do something so rehearsed

by the living? Can a girl
made of ice ever do
anything but melt?

They told you this
is where your story ends.

She had other plans.

No ballroom is ever big
enough for her.
No story is long enough. No life

is lived enough. You could
save her, you know.
The forever damsel

who has never needed

saving. There is honey in
her heart and a pirate beneath

her feet. With coffee on
her teeth she tells you stories
of the life you wanted; the

doors you wish you'd walked through.

She is the daughter of explorers.
Fate and time woven into one
collection of bones and blood.

This is the story she sculpted
from magic and madness.

And this is not the epilogue.

OUR OWN RENAISSANCE

Recall the history of the ages and how our ancestors taught
the sun to dance. We made this history known.

Painters of our own Renaissance. *Girlhood is a spectrum*
they say. Reduce us to clouds in coffee mugs—hot

to the touch. We're something to consume. We covered
the heat warning, daring the world to sue us

for burning. And I dared you to run away
with me. Become pirates. Become legendary. Watch the oil

paintings run in the rain. Smeared memories. Abandoned
ideas—novels in our minds, odes and epics trapped

behind our eyes. But no ice age or insurmountable
passage of time can make me forget the taste

of butterbeer on my tongue and that picture
perfect smile on your face.

NOT AND NEVER ELEANOR

Some say magic is wanting something and letting yourself have it. Some say the ship sank many years ago and we're just drowning— I'm drowning. Are rabbits strong swimmers? I was never entirely sure. For all the books I read I was truly as ignorant as they come when it came to the world around me. The pillars and the dollhouse and the burned place and the door that led to a forever I was never allowed to have. Rabbits can represent fertility. Abundance. Good luck. The last one is a joke. I should miss her more than I do. I shouldn't have waited for him as long as I did.

If I wish each piece into perfection every time it breaks, then does my ship remain the same through and through? Honey soaked and forever cursed. Would Theseus be proud of me? (I read about him in a book once).

How long is forever, do you think? A moment or a lifetime? What defines a lifetime anyway? The number of hands you allow to hold you, or the number of dances you dare to dance, or the way wine tastes right after you've popped the cork? The stories told you I was a rabbit. But I was an explorer long before I was anything else and now I am again. I think I was supposed to be exploring all along.

The boy with the broken heart, he's your person, isn't he?

I had a person once. I had warm hands and frantic kisses from a beautiful mouth.

I had forever for just a moment.
Now I have the sea for life.

YESTERDAYS

he says he doesn't care. mushroom tea
and stale cakes. a card game
that goes as long as the clock ticks
and this is what happens when
you murder
time.

this is how your bones
wilt and your heart
breaks and the world
cracks open like an egg
around you, the yolk
running like sunshine-yellow blood.
yet he waits.
waits for the sound of her blue dress.
for the smell of her candy-scented

hair. for a day
when he can smash the clock
and curse the hour he's had to live
over and over. full of riddles
with no answers and songs
with no melodies and madness
with no reprieve.

he waits for the day
when she will come back.
a return like the changing
of the seasons. her voice, the sound

of beginnings. their tomorrows
tastes like yesterdays.

he tilts his hat down over

his eyes. the clock ticks.
and he waits.

but he'd know her anywhere.

SUNG BY A MADMAN OR A FOOL

The Summers are coming!
Dancing with crowns full of daisies,
eye full of begonias, lungs full—

of ragweed. Sing! Sing
for the summer spirits and their while-o-the-wisp
ways. The country girl with her honey-jar-hands—
country boy waiting
for a Junebug wedding day.

Adelais! Adelais!

Who knows if she wanted
to go. A French wedding, fleur-de-lys
in her hair. The gardens
in Amboise became a Chateau
in the faeries' minds. Sing!

Adalais, what a pretty, tea-party-
bride she made. The country boy became
a doormouse, an Englishman sang
a song, and so so so it goes, the sad sad song of Adalais.

VASILISA

I went out into the snow to find
you. And you were
there, loud like a beating
heart. Come to me–
I begged.
I long to be the stuff
of stories–the witch
of the wood, with snow
bells in her hair, long past
their dying bloom.
But you are melting under the high summer heat. Midnight
and Midday are snipping
the lives of holy men
like thread.
But who
better
to love a devil than a damned
witch-girl, wanton and unwanted.
Could you
love me?
Because, as I could–

OWL KING

The kind of men that walk on moors, walked off the pages of plays she
never remembered the words to.

She's not afraid of you.

And wasn't that the problem all along?

You were offered a faerie throne in name only.
Your mother took St. John's Wort and pixies' bloom,

pressed them to your palm for luck. Like a child
you knew nothing of the magic pulsing all around you.

The air was so thick with it, it's a wonder you didn't
choke. Some call you

kobold, some say changeling, but you're the very
workings of this story. It's stitched into your skin.

She sees a magician. Cloaks and shadows. Pretty lies and ugly truths.
The creatures know

you're a heralder of death. Your gloved hands burn

from the fruit you know you can't have. Fruit you
know she'll never eat.
If she had to choose, why on earth would it be you?

If the meaning has already floated

to the surface,

why do you still
focus
on the details?

The way she smiles when she forgets
you're looking. The way her hair smells

coated in the sunrise-scented dust of your
maze. How can a palace so full, feel so empty?
This is what you wanted. A way out. Curse
the curse and forget. Walk into the light
of the machinery and damn the past.
Erase the ballroom and let the paintings run—

turning them into streams of memories you don't dare hold
on to.

She's not in the ballroom. So you're cursed
to remember her.

You have spent too long trying to be the wicked thing living inside her
storybooks. The being
worthy of her heroine monologue.
You became her Owl King, through and through.

You stumbled into this world on faerie feet
with magic flowers in your hands
and a Venetian heart in your chest
and have wondered all this time why

this place wasn't made for you. A satyr-stormed palace and faerie throne
for a man with clockwork in his
bones.

You have no power
over her.

But you love her, still.
And that has been the problem all along.

OUR TRAGEDY

ACT ONE
I don't have a name, but I'm real enough.
I *feel* real. I can smell the stink
of your gin and the sweat from your skin
and I can hear the music
in your walls. You
didn't dream me here. I saw you—
second
avenue. Clear skies, and gray hearts.
You room is a rabbit hole
and I've fallen. Do I seem ghost
enough for you?
I can help you get back to the stars.
We can build a rocket ship made
up of stuff and nonsense. Your
words and my songs, and it can
take you home.

ACT TWO
I was real once. Cut down in my prime.
Not properly dead. Not fully a ghost.
I could be so much
more if I learned how to die.
I didn't come here to teach
you how to live.
I'm here to help you escape
the cruel joke
of the dying man who can't die.
We could end together. Turn

our tragedy
into a tale of epic

48

heroes.
We could make more out
of the drawing of a rocket ship
on your floor.

You could crawl up inside
of it, and with my hands on your
heart we could get lost in these stars.
Just speak some more,
and we'll travel on.

BAKCHEIA

You're telling me You saw god. how am i
supposed to swallow those words like
all the other ones

you told me? i can't make
biblical baskets and send these quiet
thoughts floating down the river. i can't let

the snow bury them only to thaw when
spring comes. when wise words arrive
years from now to tell me

that this was all a mistake. *You* were
a mistake. You said you all wore
chitons and gave libations, burned hemlock

and chewed laurel leaves. this is not
an urban legend—You are not a myth
in the making. this is just school and You are

just a man. the moon can shine
blindingly on anyone who dares
think themselves worthy. dante or dionysus,

it doesn't matter who You saw or what You
heard. all i see is the blood. all i feel is the pain.
i've never reached a state of euphoria, so maybe

i'll never see god. but i've seen You,
and maybe for now that is enough.
or maybe for always.

DEATH CAP

He's as gray as the skies that haunt this forest. This academic town. This rich kid cucumber sandwich, popping champagne in cemeteries type of place. We could all choke on any

thing he asked us to. Drink moonlight, or shoot it up into our veins.

This is what the gods wanted. But some get too slick. Too high
on the feeling of being wanted.
Needed.
Loved.
We don't love here.

Loose lips sink ships and the water is already too rough for how seriously he's rocking the boat.

So god will cut him down.
God—*our* god—wears ties and blazers. Speaks in a false greek-coated tongue and his love language is picking up the tab. Pouring the wine. Smiling unsettling smiles. Telling you you're just like him.
I don't know if that's a bad thing.

But for this white rabbit in our midst it most certainly is.
One side of the mushroom
makes you bigger and one side makes you small.

And if our false god can get enough, we can kill
the rabbit. Make him drop dead. Stop his ticking heart and have him
for dinner. A feast fit for kings.

NOT ABLE TO DIE OR LEAVE

We fly by falling.
Gin and milk
to mend. King and Queen.

I'll drink and you'll lie
and we'll shake our fists
at the stars. And they'll come

from all corners
of the woods. Beating
their chests, blood on their fists.

We may not be able
to die, but we can beat them.

                           Just today.

This isn't safe. We both
know you should leave
me. Climb

back up the rabbit hole
and forget all of this.

I'm sorry, but—
you could stay. I could be

King and you could be Queen.
and we could buzz louder

than bees. Love wilder than the woods. We could just be.

               We're heroes today. Just today.

SINCE THOU WILT NOT REMAIN HERE

I hear her feet on the mossy ground,
early, early. Just listening.
At this hour there
is only the sea
sounds. *Wait*

for me, she calls out to a boy
named something from a legend
once told around fires
full of lion's roars.
But now, she's
surrounded

by loam and lichen. The birds are
on their way. Sunlight dripping from
their wings; looking for
the great queen or
goddess. She

doesn't see them or hear them as
they wake the dead. *You will never
come back,* the legend-
boy calls to her. She
does not hear
him over

the sound of the sea.
Only Mabinoagion knows her now.

A PIECE OF PAPER FOUND TUCKED UNDER A MUSHROOM DEEP IN THE FOREST

He never forgets what it tastes
like to love her. Peaches

and winter teeth,
he bites her till
she bleeds and she

savors the sound of his mouth—
calling her name.
His love for her rattles the stars.
Her love for him shatters
them all one by one.

> The sky was never darker
> then the day they fell
> in love.

UNTIL I AM SICK OF IT

The crown fits you too well. I fit you too well.
Handing over my rowan berries and salt. Licking your lips without fairy
fruit to tempt me and jeerers to taunt me.

You're better than me–
only because I worked so hard to be so much worse.

The winds bar me now. I am Queen of Nothing, and no one–

owes me
anything.

And do you know what it is like to love a wicked thing?

BITTERSWEET

He came to me during a long night. Snow-soaked trees and warm hands.
I had never thought about endings

before him. It made sense to think less
of storms. Fear them less. Chase fireflies more. He said I

had so much to learn. So much to achieve.

Over iced coffees, years after school had ended, he gave me sad looks;
weary eyes. I'd lost

my muchness. I'd dared
to walk through this forest on my own. Towards the cottage where they
say the witches work. I hadn't looked back, hand outstretched, waiting
for him. The schoolgirl, always in need.

The longer I think about his lemon eyes and mint tongue, his scruffy
beard, and curly hair,
the more I remember of how little I learned.

He didn't tell me which berries were
poisonous. I learned that on my own. I can pick them

now, safe for my baking, because I knew enough to know I needed to
learn how to survive.

Warm hands are comforting in the winter, but blazing once the sun
returns.

I am burning. I am no longer a schoolgirl.

I don't want to stay in his forest forever. I can reach the cottage on
my own.

I have a basketful of stories I spun myself, made up of fears all my own. I
became the wanderer he hoped each one of us girls would never learn

how to be. He is the kind of man who would feed you poisonous
berries

and call your dying body art. I am his

biggest failure—I was never
willing to mutilate myself for a teacher's praise.

And who was he to try and teach me what poetry tastes like, when I'm
the one who knows the names of every tree in this wood.

THE PATH THAT LEADS TO THE END

-after The Starless Sea by Erin Morgenstern

Gold and blue paint on bricks
the color of blood. You roll

one of each and wait for the mad
hatter, but I'm afraid you're in the wrong

story. We wish we had a happier
ending for you this time; wish we could

makes the pages honey-sweet.

but you know
the way. The blade is sharp
enough and your heart beats
loud enough. You can outrun

the flap of wings and you know
how to swim.

We're quite fond of you, you know.
So we're rooting for you.
You know all the stories. you memorized
all the tales of times gone by.

The rabbit is waiting for you.
When you find her, know that we are proud
of you, son of the fortune teller.
We are proud you finally figured out
how the story ends.

RABBIT HOLES ARE NOT ALWAYS RABBIT HOLES

i've been looking for you in peeled
apple skins. you're faded—

> you're not who you were when
> the caterpillar sat on the mushroom

and the bottle said *drink me*
and all his hands made you forget.

who you were supposed to be.

CANABILIZE THE WARMEST SEASON

Cannibalize the Warmest Season

Grow from the wild
weeds they pretended were strangling
you. There is no
vigor in her words. No mettle in his.
There is nothing inside
their bones but dust.

(Fee fi fo fum)

They thought themselves giant.
Important.
Meaningful.
Great means so many things in so many
different mouths. Even vipers can
hiss words into existence.

(A plague of snakes)

Bloody steaks made of hearts,
line dinner tables at parties
you didn't know
they were having.
Swallow the summer sun
and call it a day.

Make art from all the broken
windows—shattered from their storms.

(A happy ending)

WELCOME HOME

The Hazel tree at the center of the woods is just
a rumor. The witches made it up to tell scared little children. Warn

them to be wary of what lurks
in the dark of day, and the moonlight
of night.

And most of the children
listened.
Not you.

You grew up with mischief
in your blood and goblin
stories in your brain and you wished

for a magic you could
taste and feel and know
and become.

You've gone into the woods.
Encountered the widow at the stone
and the melancholy king on

his meaningless faerie throne.
You've danced with the damned
and tasted the honey

of the misfit sailed sea beneath
our feet. You have called the ancient storyteller
by name and looked

into the eyes of the reckless
dancing and dreaming of Gods

they'll never know.

You've survived the menacing
mushrooms and the honey-coated
bee-brewed wine and mead.

You have known everything
there is to know long before
you braved our branches

and our deadly copse
and our wonderful,
horribly beautiful magic.

Put your hands on the Hazel tree.
This is where you belong.
This is where you and your ideas

and your heart and your longing finally make sense. You are not the
epilogue, you are a prologue

that has been aching to begin.
Welcome wanderer. Welcome traveler.
Welcome to the woods.

I think the best stories feel like they're still going, somewhere out in story space.

— TH STARLESS SEA BY ERIN MORGENSTERN

Acknowledgments

This book was a passion project that is near and dear to our hearts, and we feel has been a proper peek into our souls. But we couldn't have done it without some support and inspiration. We'd like to thank the brilliant Erin Morgenstern for writing our favorite book *The Starless Sea* that has inspired so much of this book, and ultimately changed our lives for the better. Molly would like to thank her mother and sister for always supporting her writing and having faith in her. Mar would like to thank Defne Cizakca for being a source of inspiration and the best mentor and friend one could have hoped for. She would also like to thank Leticia Olguín and Alfredo Ruiz, for surrounding her with magic and art and for always having her back. We'd like to thank you. To everyone who read this book and supported us, we want to thank you for going on this journey with us through the woods into this world we created and wove together from our favorite stories and bits of our hearts and souls. Thank you for reading. Thank you for believing. We can only hope that our collection of poetry and art has brought just a little bit more magic into your lives. And lastly, we'd like to thank the bees.

About the Authors

Deep in the woods and down a rabbit hole you will find a theatrical poet trying to make sense of this great, vast world. Molly Likovich is the best-selling author of *Riding The Headless Horseman* and has also penned romantic titles such as *Send in The Clowns* and *Getting With The Ghoul*. She has a BA in Creative Writing from Salisbury University and her poetry and short stories have appeared in *Rust + Moth, Shore Poetry,* and *Love Letters to Poe Vol. 3* among others. She is currently sailing the Starless Sea and breathing the haunted air.

Behind a cloud of incense and the steam rising from a cup, you can find a witch concocting enchanting things. Marcia Ruiz-Olguín, writer, jeweler and illustrator, with a Creative Writing certificate from The University of Edinburgh and a BA in Literature from Universidad de las Américas Puebla. She dwells in a corner of this world surrounded by pirates, gods of old and her two shadows Kara and Luna.

Also by Molly & Mar

The Willow's Silence

The Fable of Wonderland